Mies van der Rohe

Villa Tugendhat
1930

世界遺産

トゥーゲントハット邸
1930　チェコ
ミース・ファン・デル・ローエ

トゥーゲントハット邸の十字柱断面。
Section of the Cross-shaped column, Villa Tugendhat

Credits
©Kyouji Morimoto
  5 right, 7bottom right, 8-9 all, 10 both, 13, 16, 17 above right, 18 both, 23 bottom right, 24 both, 32 above right, 33 right, 52 top
©Jin Kurita
  7 above right, 25 bottom, 30 left, 35 left, 52 bottom
©Museum of the City of Brno
  37 all, 53
©Bauhaus-Archiv Berlin
  portrait
All other photographs Kazuyoshi Miyamoto©

トゥーゲントハット邸
Villa Tugendhat

目 次

- ◇住宅写真 — 4-27
- ◇図面 — 32-37, 42-43
- ◇ディティール — 28-31
- ◇「モダニズムの白い聖書」
  - 住宅の形をした"Less is more"
  - ブルノへの道 — 38
  - 満身創痍の名住宅 — 38
  - 創建時の姿に復元、そして世界遺産へ — 44
  - 出生地の地政学的座標 — 44
  - 「ミース起元元年」、同時代の建築家たち — 46
  - モダニストたちの共通点 — 48
  - イメージを実現する突出した建設費 — 50
  - "Less is more"の一頂点 — 54

Contents

- ◇Photos of the Villa Tugendhat — 4-27
- ◇Drawings — 32-37, 42-43
- ◇Details — 28-31
- ◇White Bible of Modernism
  - "Less is More" in the Shaping of Housing
  - Road to Brno — 39
  - Superb Residence with Scattered Wounds — 39
  - Restored to the Original Shape and to Be on the World Heritage List — 45
  - Geopolitical Position of Mies' Birthplace — 45
  - Mies Era, Architects of the Same Period — 47
  - Common Ground for Modernists — 49
  - Outstanding Construction Fees to Realize Images — 51
  - Peak of "Less is More" — 55

▲ トゥーゲントハット邸の東側のファサード。ブルノ中心市街地からタクシーで10分ほどのなだらかな坂の上に位置する、周辺は住宅地。白の外壁、陸屋根の外観は、周囲の勾配屋根にアースカラーの外壁の住宅群中にあって、創建当時どれほど奇異の目で見られたことだろう。

Eastern façade of the Villa Tugendhat. It is about 10 minutes by taxi from the center of Brno city and is located on a gentle slope in a residential area. The white-walled villa with its flat roof stands out amidst the surrounding earth-colored houses with their pitched rooflines. How strange has it may be seemed at its completion?

▲ 南東外観。道路側から、この住宅の巨大さはほとんどわからない。
Southeast appearance. It is difficult to discern the massiveness of the villa.

▲ 玄関脇の乳白色半透明壁面。地階に向かう「半らせん階段」が内部にある。黒く見える方立がオリジナル。原設計の黒い方立の間にあるスチールの細い方立は、戦後の補修で追加された部分。

Half transparent, milky white walls beside the entrance. Inside, there is a "strand stairway" to the underground floor. The black mullions are original. The thin steel mullions between the original black ones were added at the postwar renovation.

▲ 表庭から西側の庭園への通り抜け。左側が住宅、右側が従業員室と車庫。現在はミュージアムショップ。

Passage from the front garden to the west garden. On the left side is the villa and on the right, the servants' room and a garage. These are now used as a museum shop.

▲ 1階西面、主寝室のバルコニー。低い手摺壁が不思議に怖さを感じさせない。
Western side of the balcony off the main bedroom on the 1st floor. Surprisingly, this low balustrade does not look out of place.

▲「半らせん階段」のガラス壁を半周回り込んだ奥に玄関扉。
Entrance door is half way around the glass wall of the "strand stairway."

▲子供室前の廊下から「半らせん階段」方向を見る。
Looking towards the "strand stairway" from the hallway before the children's room.

▲ 玄関を入って振り返ったところ。非常に明るいが、柔らかい上品な光に溢れている。細く見える方立が戦後の改修で取付けられたもの。ガラスはエッチング加工により"milk glass"と呼ばれる状態になっている。オリジナルは1枚が幅2.3m、高さ3mでエッチング加工。半らせん階段部分はそれに曲面加工が加わり、高価格な部材。左が玄関扉。

Looking back from the entrance. Very bright, full of gentle light. Thin mullions were attached at the postwar renovation. The style of etched glass here is called "milk glass." The original etched glass plate is 2.3m wide and 3m high. The glass for the strand stairway, where the glass is even curved, is of an expensive material. On the left side is the entrance door.

▲ 子供部屋西側バルコニーに面する開口。開き扉と
窓には別々にブラインドが屋外に組込まれている。
*The window and the door to the balcony of the children's room facing west.
The blind is installed outside for the door and the window.*

▲ 子供部屋の外側。市街地方向を眺める大きなバルコニーに半円形のベンチ。
Outside the children's room. Semicircular bench in the large balcony facing the city.

▲ 主寝室ゾーンのバスルーム。夫婦それぞれに洗面器を持つのは、それぞれの茶碗や歯ブラシを持つのと同じ、という欧州人の衛生意識。

Bathroom for the main bedroom. In accordance with the concept of Western personal hygiene separate sinks are deemed as necessary as separate cups or toothbrushes.

◀ 奥から、浴槽、便器、ビデ、洗面器という構成。反対側にスチーム暖房の放熱器。頂側窓採光により非常に明るい空間となっている。

From back to front, bathtub, lavatory sink, bidet and washing sink, There is a heat radiator on the other side. The high side window makes this area very light.

▲ 半らせん階段の下部。足元にスチーム暖房の放熱器が装備され、竪穴部分の寒さを防ぐ。
Bottom of the strand stairway. There is a steam-heat radiator to mitigate the coldness of the vertical shaft.

▲ 玄関扉の隣接部分、地階へ降りる「半らせん階段」の上部。面積の大きなガラス面からの熱損失を防ぐため、ガラス面の下部、円筒形の壁の上部にスチーム暖房の放熱パイプを設置。

The adjoining area of the entrance door is above the "strand stairway" to the downstairs. There is a steam-heated radiation pipe between the cylindrical wall and glass to decrease the heat loss from the large glass surface.

▲ 地下1階に降りて、居間・食堂部分に至る導入部分。ダイニングルームを囲む半円形をしたマカッサル黒檀の隔壁の背中側が見える。

Basement floor, front chamber of the dining and living room. The back of the bulkhead wall made of Makassar ebony wood, can be seen in a semicircle which surrounds the dining room.

14-15頁の見返しの眺め、南方向。正面にグランドピアノのある書斎ゾーン越しに奥行き2.6mの温室ゾーン。無垢のオニックス壁面の右側は居間。
South direction of the area on page 14 and 15. The conservatory has a depth of 2.6m and is behind the reading area, which has a grand piano. Behind the pure onyx wall is the living room.

▲ 幅2.6m、奥行き14.5m、シダ系、ゴムノキ系の観葉植物が一年中リビングから望める。

Width 2.6m and Depth 14.5m. You can see foliage plants such as ferns and rubber trees, all year round from the living room.

▶ 書斎ゾーンからガラススクリーン越しに温室を見る。こちら側が南面。鉢をのせる台の下に、スチーム暖房のラジエーターが水平に設置されている。

Looking towards the conservatory from the reading area through the glass screen. The foreground is south. A steam-heat radiator is horizontally installed under the pot table.

▲ 書斎の東面（正面）と南面（右側）温室への出入口。
天井のペンダントはポールヘニングセンの「PH4 1/2-4」。
左手の椅子はブルノ・チェア。右手の椅子は肘掛ありの
「MRチェア」。

The doorway of the reading room to the east (straight ahead) and the south (to the right). The pendant light from the ceiling is "PH4 1/2-4" by Paul Henningsen. You can see Brno chairs on the left and "MR chairs" with armrests on the right.

▲ オニックス壁の西側、居間の領域。正面が南、右手が西、遙かに中心市街地を見下ろす。ソファはこの住宅のためにデザインされたトゥーゲントハット・チェア。テーブルを挟んで向う側にバルセロナ・チェア。彫刻は、ヴィルヘルム・レームブルック作の「見返り娘」。

The west side of the onyx wall is the living room. Straight ahead is south and to the right is west. The central part of the city can be seen in the distance. The sofa is a Tugendhat chair, designed for this residence. There are Barcelona chairs behind the table. The sculpture is "Looking back Girl" by Wilhelm Lehmbruck.

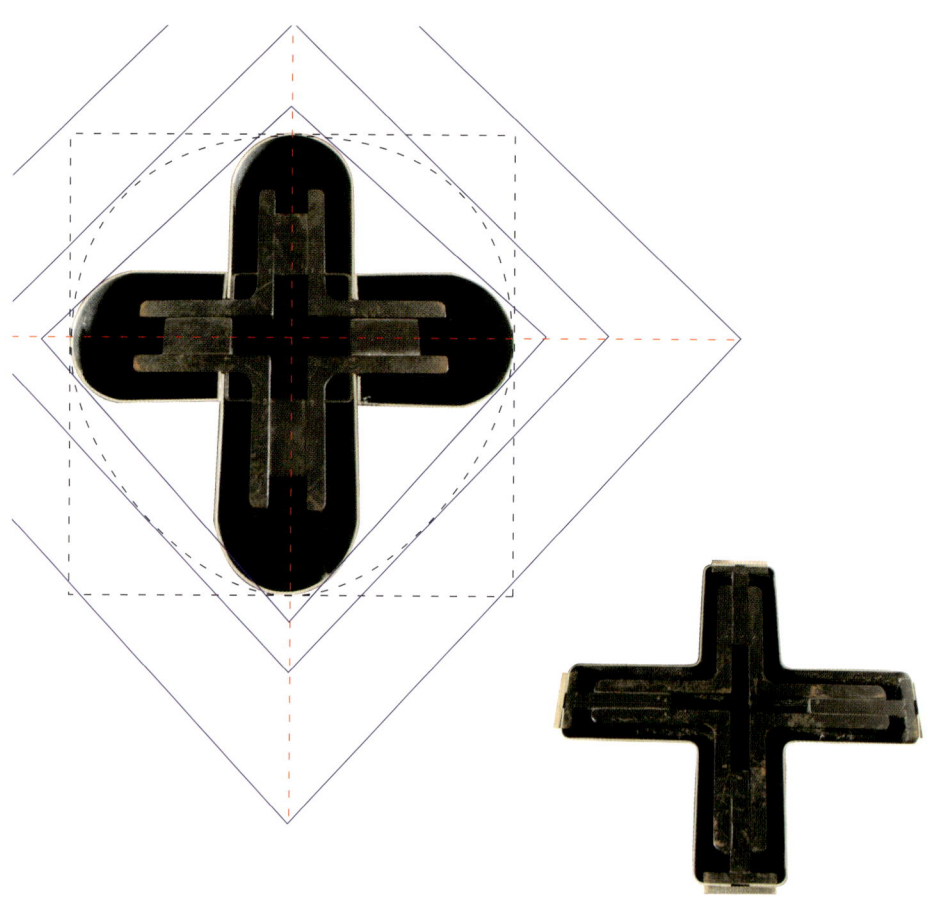

東京大学　工学部建築学科蔵
バルセロナ・パビリオン、トゥーゲントハット邸「スターコラム」のための断面試作

Collection of Department of Architecture, Faculty of Engineering, the University of Tokyo
Barcelona Pavilion, trial section for the "star column" of the Villa Tugendhat

左：トゥーゲントハット邸　独立柱
右：バルセロナ・パヴィリオン　独立柱

ミースは、独立柱として、エジプト、ギリシア以来のトラディショナルな円柱を採用したくなかった。近代建築のパイオニアとしての矜持であろう。さらに、正面から見ても斜めから見ても、柱の太さが最大41％も変わってしまう角柱を避けたい。そこで、十字柱なら、柱としてのX、Y双方向に関する断面性能を維持できる。そして、眺める角度によって柱の太さに変化が少ない十字型断面に加え、膨らんで（円に近づく）ケーシングという構成とした。バルセロナ・パヴィリオンの柱より、見た目に優しい。

Left: Villa Tugendhat, Column
Right: Barcelona Pavilion, Column

Mies did not like to use traditional cylindrical columns from the Egyptian and Greek age, probably because he prided himself in being a pioneer of modern architecture. In addition, he wanted to avoid the rectangular columns as the apparent width of the columns changes by 41% depending on where you look at them. Therefore, he chose cross-shaped columns, which can sustain cross-section performance and the apparent width of the columns do not change much with ones viewing angle. Besides, by adopting a casing composition, which swells to a circle these columns look softer than the ones of the Barcelona Pavilion.

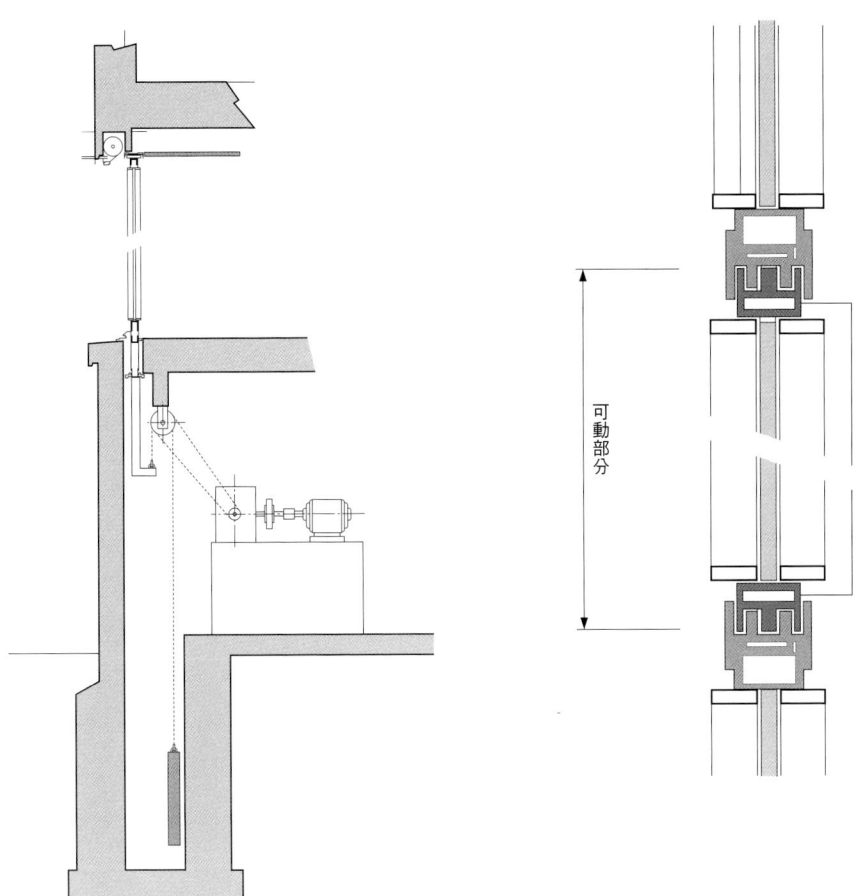

左：居間窓の金引込み部分の断面図
右：断面詳細図

左：地下2階の電動窓用機械室に設けられたモーターから、ギャドライブで駆動プーリーを回し、そこから上階近くに設けられた窓の駆動装置まで、ベルトドライブで伝達する仕組み。
右：可動部分の隙間風対策として、引戸の鴨居の桶端のような3本溝の断面を方立側に用意している。

Section (left) and detailed section (right) of the retracting parts of the living room window

Left: Turning the drive pulley by the gear drive at the motor installed in the mechanical room for the retracting window on the 2nd basement floor. The device transmits force by the belt drive to the window drive apparatus.
Right: The section of the mullion with 3 ditches like a sliding door track is to prevent draft at the movable parts.

▲ ブルノ市東部のなだらかな西下がりの斜面の景色を借景とするフルハイトの開口部。「高さ3.17m、幅2.4mの1枚ガラス×2枚の構成」の巨大なガラス面が一つおきに電動仕掛けで地下2階に引き込まれ、室内が外部の景色と完全に一体化する様は壮観。

Full-height window with scenery of eastern Brno, in the background, gently sloping down towards the west.
One can enjoy the marvelous integration of the interior and exterior views when every other plate of huge glass, "3.17m (height) × 2.4m (wide)" is retracted by electricity into the 2nd basement floor.

▲ 居間ゾーンの南西隅角部。十字型断面の独立柱（列柱）は、南北方向のスパンが4.9m東西方向のスパンが5.5mで、クロームめっきしたブロンズ板を巻いている。表面に周囲の景色を映し込み、柱の存在感を薄める。

Reentrant angle of the southeast part of the living room. Cross-shaped columns, rolled by bronze sheets with chrome coating, are located at intervals of 4.9m (north-to-south axis) and 5.5m (east-to-west). The surfaces of the columns reflect the surrounding scenery and downplay the actual presence of the columns.

▲ 居間ゾーンから北面を望む。可動ガラススクリーンの外部に、地下1階（居間階）から西側の庭園に降りる大理石の階段が見える。

Looking towards the north from the living room. You can see stairs of marble towards the west garden at the basement level (living room floor) beside the retractable glass screen.

地下1階のテラス。食堂ゾーンのドアから外に出る。右側、居間の大型のガラス開口部は、手前から2番目と4番目のガラススクリーンが下階にスライドする。

Terrace on the basement floor. There is an entrance from the dining room. Regarding the large windows, to the right, the 2nd and the 4th glass screens from the foreground slide down.

▲ 地下1階のテラスから北側を望む。右側に見える窓は使用人住居部分の厨房西面開口部。
Looking towards the north from the terrace on the basement floor. The western window of the servants' kitchen area on the right can be seen.

24

↑ 幅6.8m、奥行き9.8mの堂々たるスケールのテラス。
Magnificent terrace of 6.8m (width) × 9.8m (depth).

← 庭に降りる幅4.7mの階段。ドイツ敗戦後、この家を接収したロシアの軍隊は、この階段を馬で上り下りしたという話がある。

4.7m wide stairs going down to the garden. An anecdote says that the Russian army, which took over the villa after the German defeat of the war, went up and down these stairs on horses

敷地の傾斜がわかる南側外観。地下1階「南面の水平連続開口」と、地上1階は乳母室の窓、地下2階の多目的室の窓が見える。

Sloping south appearance. You can see the "continuum of horizontal windows on the south" on the basement floor, the windows of the nanny's room on the ground floor and the windows of the multipurpose room on the 2nd basement floor.

▲ 雪の積もった西斜面の庭園から、トゥーゲントハット邸の西側および右側に東側（温室側）の外観を見る。

Western and eastern (conservatory) of the Villa Tugendhat from the garden on the snowy hill to the west.

▲ 地下1階のテラスから望む庭園の冬景色。遠景に大木の枝越しにブルノの中心市街地。

Winter view of the garden from the terrace on the basement floor. Central Brno can be seen through branches in the distance.

Detail - 1

トゥーゲントハット邸では、現在3種類のレバー・ハンドルが見られる。左は乳母室窓の線の細いレバーハンドル、右は子供部屋からテラスへの出入口。その他の扉には直角に曲げた角棒と丸棒の組合せのシンプルなものを使用。

There are now 3 kinds of lever handles at the Villa Tugendhat. The left side is a thin lever handle for the nanny's room and the right side is for a doorway from the children's room to the terrace. A simple combination of a square bar bended at right angles and a round bar is used for other doors.

上:片開き扉のドア・ストッパー。手前側の「碇」でドアを捕える。ローレット加工した中央部を靴で回転させるとドアが解放される仕掛けとなっている。
右:子供部屋の収納部(左)と廊下に通じる扉(右)。扉の表面材は他の造作部分に揃えた黒檀の練り付け。

Top: Door stopper for a single swing door. The "anchor" at the foreground captures the door. You can release the door by rolling the knurled middle part with a shoe.
Right: Storage (left) and the door to the hallway (right) in the children's room. The surface wood of the door is ebony like the other ornamental parts.

Detail - 2

左上：地下1階、中央が居間部分のガラスを地下2階に引き込む部分。
右上：テラス（p24上）から見る使用人住居部分の厨房窓。
左下：地下1階の北西外観。画面右側（西面）、4連の窓の内、手前から2番目と4番目が電動でそっくり地下2階に引き込まれる。

Top Left: Basement floor. The part where the glass of the living room is retracted into the 2nd basement floor.
Top Right: Kitchen room window of the servants' area looking from the terrace (p.24 top).
Bottom Left: Northwestern appearance. The 2nd and the 4th of the 4 windows in the right (west side) are fully retracted into the 2nd basement floor.

● 左：窓が完全開口となり、外部には地下2階外部の地面と約3mの落差ができるゆえに手摺が必須。角パイプのクロームメッキ仕上げ。
右：手摺の足元には、同じくクロームメッキ仕上げのフットレスト。実は内部にスチームを通す放熱パイプでもあり、巨大ガラス面のコールド・ドラフト除けの役目を果たしている。

Left: A guardrail is a must because the window can be fully opened and the room is 3m higher than the ground. A square pipe is coated with chrome.
Right: Footrests, located below the guardrail, are also chrome coated. They are actually radiation pipes as well with steam running through them. These pipes function so that there won't be cold drafts on this huge glass surface.

平面図／Floor plans

Fisrt plans

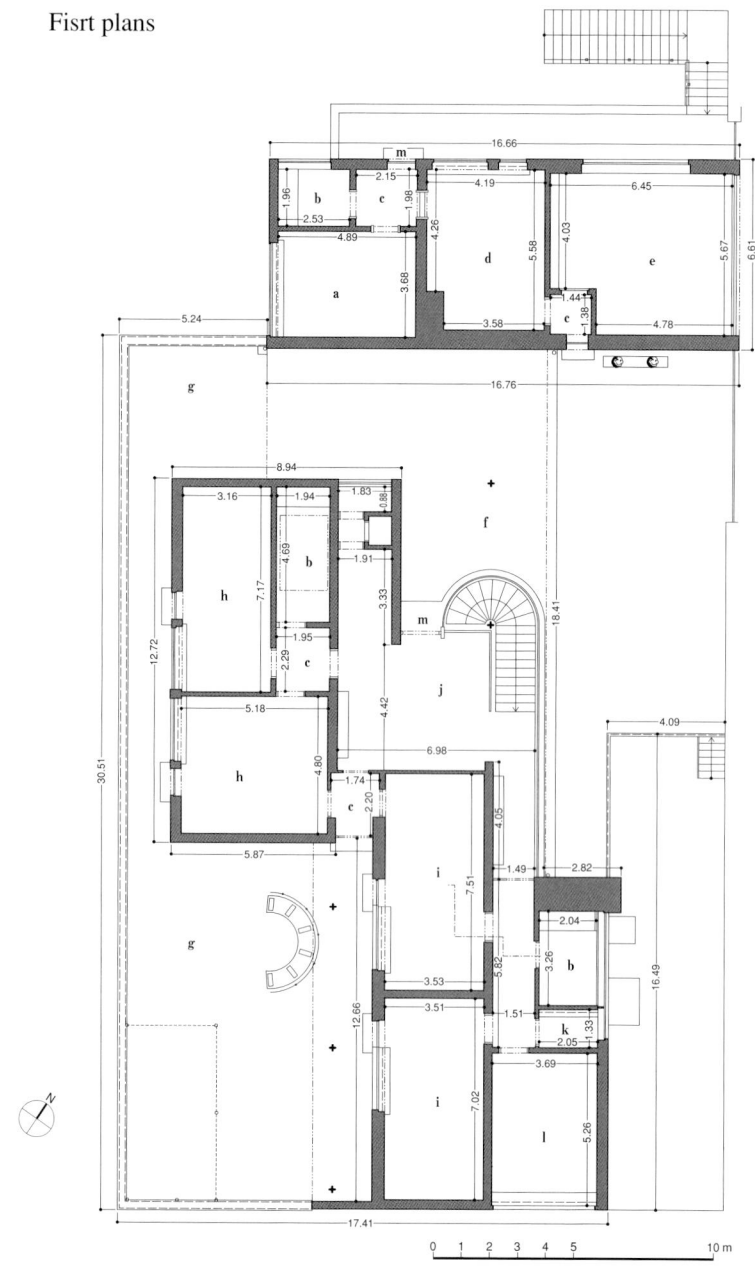

a. 使用人台所 b. 浴室 c. 前室 d. 居室 e. ガレージ f. ポーチ
g. テラス h. 主寝室 i. 子供室 j. ホール k. WC l. 乳母室 m. 玄関

a. servants' kitchen b. bathroom c. front chamber d. room e. garage f. porch
g. terrace h. main bedroom i. children's room j. hall k. WC l. nanny's room m. entrance

Ground plans

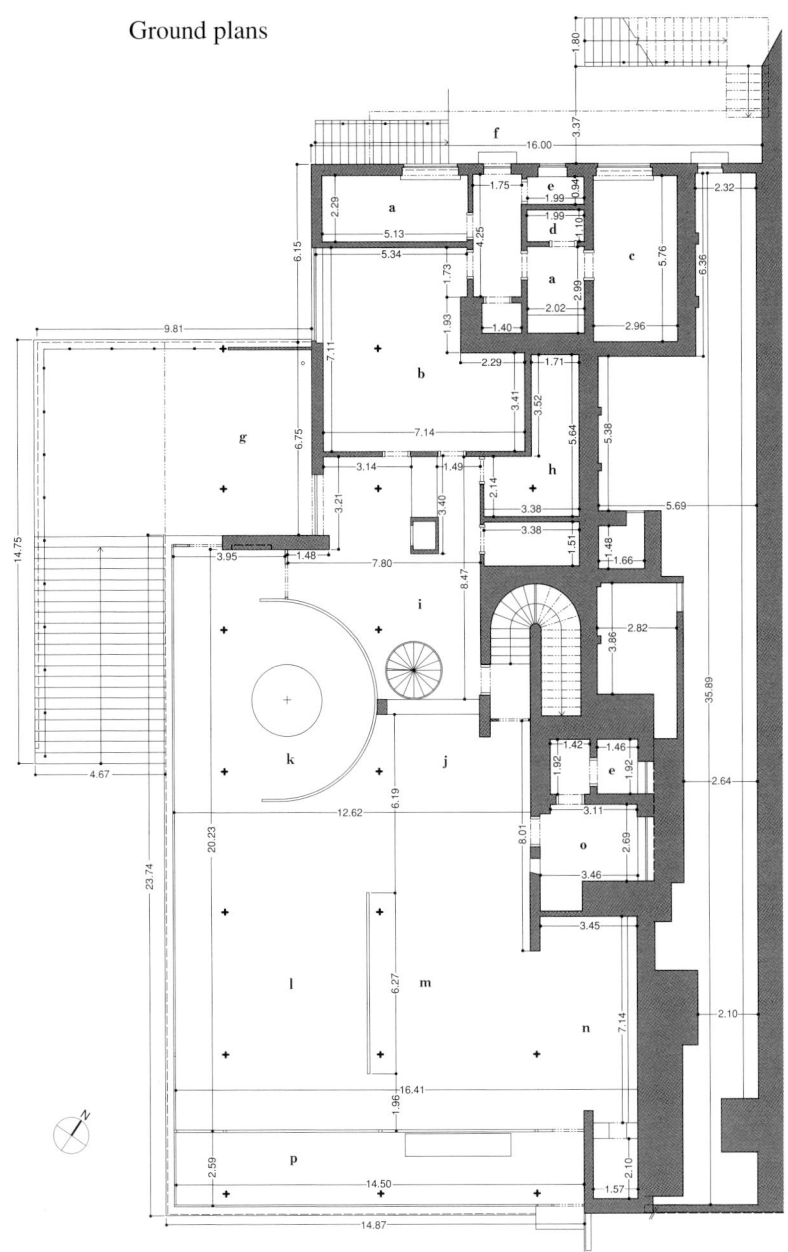

a. 物入れ b. 厨房 c. 使用人居間 d. 浴室 e. WC f. 使用人用玄関
g. テラス h. 倉庫 i. 配膳室 j. ホール k. 食堂 l. 居間 m. 書斎 n. 図書館 o. 映写室 p. 温室
*a. storage b. kitchen c. servants' living room d. bathroom e. WC f. servants' entrance
g. terrace h. storage i. butler's pantry j. reception hall k. dining room l. living room m. reading
room n. library o. projection room p. conservatory*

Basement

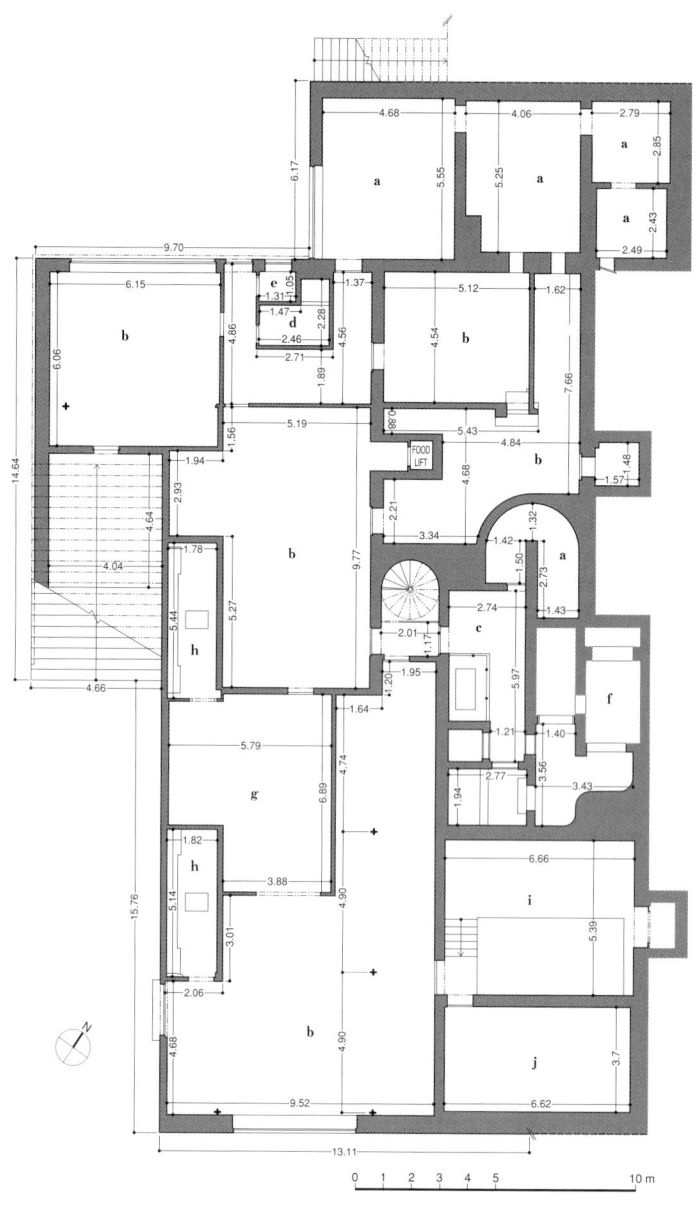

a. 倉庫　b. 多目的室　c. 機械室　d. シャワー室　e. WC　f. 空調機械室
g. 洗濯室　h. 引込み窓の機械室　i. ボイラー室　j. セントラルヒーティング機械室
a. storage b. multipurpose room c. mechanical room d. shower room e. WC f. air-conditioning room
g. laundry room h. mechanical room with a retractable window i. boiler room j. central heating machine room

a 建設開始期の鉄骨構造、1929年
b 女性用居室、1930年
c 男性用居室、1930年

a Steel construction of the house at the beginning of building,1929
b Lady's room,1930
c Gentleman's room,1930
©Museum of the City of Brno

立面図／Elevation

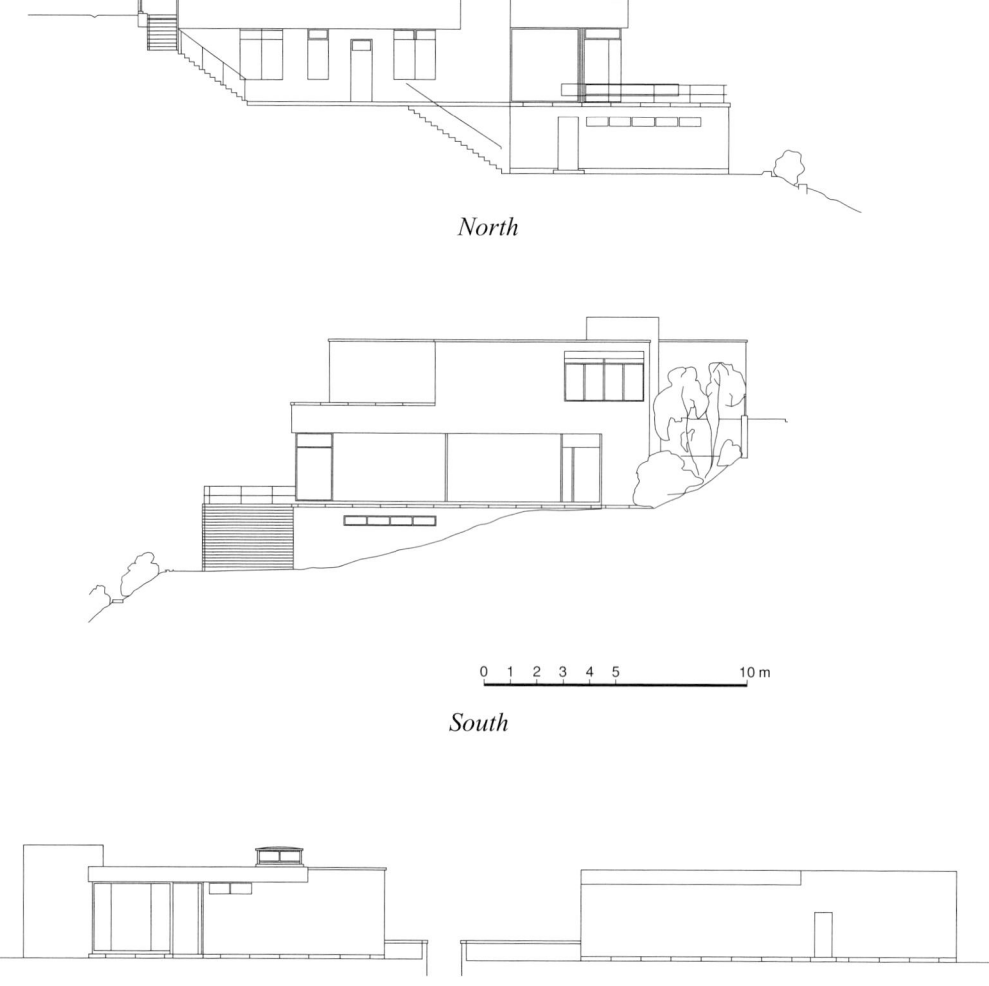

North

South

玄関ホールまわり　北側
Around the porch　North

玄関車庫・使用人住居　南側
Garage, Main residence　South

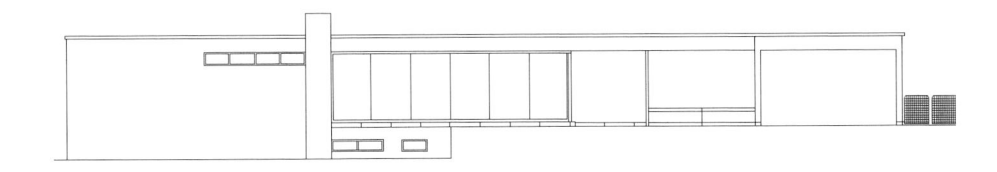

East

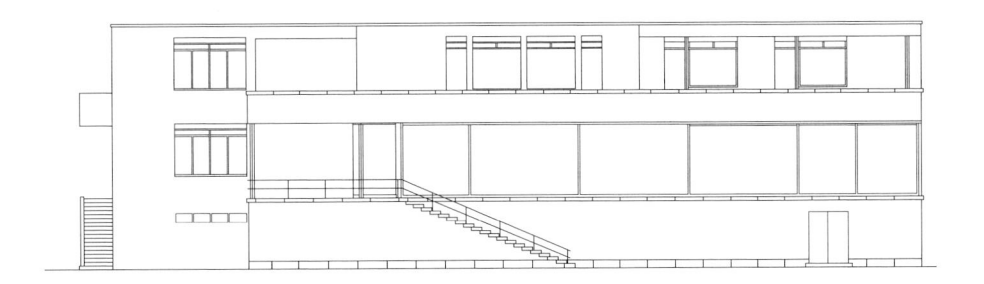

West

0 1 2 3 4 5　　10 m

トゥーゲントハット邸
建築家：ミース・ファン・デル・ローエ
竣工：1930年
主体構造：鉄骨造地上1階、地下2階建て
敷地面積：7,300m²
延床：約1,260m²
各階床面積：1F/230m²　B1F/460m²
　　　　　　B2F/570m²
住所：Černopolni 45, 61300 Brno Czech Republic

Villa Tugendhat
Architect: Mies van der Rohe
Completed in 1930
Main Structure: Steel Construction, 1 Story and 2 basement floors
Site Area: 7,300m²
Total Floor Area: about 1,260m²
Each Floor Area: 1F/230m²　B1F/460m²
　　　　　　　　B2F/570m²
Address: Černopolni 45, 61300 Brno Czech Republic

「モダニズムの白い聖書」
住宅の形をした"Less is more"

ブルノへの道

　チェコの首都プラハ最大のフロレンツ・バスターミナルから、この国第2の街、ブルノ行きのバスが出る。プラハの南東約200キロ強、高速道路を走るバスで2時間半の先にミース・ファン・デル・ローエのトゥーゲントハット邸がある。

　チェコの西半分がボヘミア、東半分がモラヴィアと呼ばれているが、ボヘミアの中心地がプラハ、モラヴィア地方の中心地(かつてのモラヴィア王国の首都)がここ、人口38万のブルノである。中心市街地は、他の地方中核都市と同様、コンパクトで、約東西800m、南北1kmの範囲に収まる。

　新市庁舎、ゴシックとバロックの様式の混じる創建14世紀の「聖ペテロ聖パウロ教会」、鉄道の「ブルノ本駅」があるあたりが低く、そこから北東方向に緩やかな丘陵を登るように住宅地が拡がっていった構成の街。

　めざすトゥーゲントハット邸は、中心市街地の周回道路から東に伸びるミラディ・ホラコブ大通りまで行き、その通りに直交して、高台の住宅地の中を北上するチェルノポルニ通りのなだらかな坂を上ると左側に見えてくる。

満身創痍の名住宅

　ミースの、代表的な住宅作品として、双壁をなすバルセロナ・パヴィリオン[※1]と、ブルノのトゥーゲントハット邸は、ほとんど同じ時期（1929年）に生み出された。当時、ミースは43歳の仕事盛りである。

　バルセロナ・パヴィリオンとトゥーゲントハット邸、近代建築の巨匠による初期の代表作は、前者はバルセロナ国際博のパヴィリオンという性格から1年に満たずに解体された。

　後者は解体されることこそ免れたが、だからといって幸せであったわけではない。社会の支配形態の変遷になすすべもなく翻弄されるという数奇な運命をたどることになった。

　ミースは、左翼から右翼まで幅広くクライアント候補者たちと交友関係を持っていた。トゥーゲントハット邸のケースは、左翼系の歴史家エードゥアルド・フックス[※2]の紹介による仕事であった。

[※1]バルセロナ・パヴィリオン
最初のプランはレンガのカントリーハウス（1923年、42頁参照）を応用したものであった。壁と独立柱を併用する第2案を経て、最終案は、8本の独立十字柱のみで支えられ、壁は非耐力の単なるスクリーンとなった。1986年に復元再建された。

[※1]**Barcelona Pavilion**
The first plan adopted the country house made of brick (1923, see p. 42). After the 2nd plan of walls and columns, the final plan was supported only by 8 cross-shaped columns and walls became a nonbearing screen. The Pavilion was reconstructed in 1986.

White Bible of Modernism
"Less is More" in the Shaping of Housing

Road to Brno

The bus to the second largest city Brno starts at the largest bus terminal, Florenc, Prague in the Czech Republic. A two and half hour highway bus drive takes you to the Villa Tugendhat by Mies van der Rohe, about 200km southeast of Prague.

The western half of the Czech Republic is called Bohemia and the eastern half Moravia. The center of Bohemia is Prague and the Moravian center is Brno with a population of 380,000, which used to be the capital of the Moravian kingdom. The central city is as compact as other regional hub cities and it is about 800m (east and west), 1km (north and south).

As for the city structure, there are Nová radnice (new city hall), Katedrála sv. Petra a Pavla (Saints Peter's and Paul's Church) built in the mixed style of Baroque and Gothic in the 14th century, Hlavní Nádrazí (main train station), and so on where the land is lower. The residential areas are spread towards the northeast on a gentle ascending slope.

You can first take the Milady Hovákové avenue running towards the east from the loop road at the center of the city. Then, go up a gentle slope of the Cernopolni street that lies at right angles to the avenue running through residential areas towards the north and you will see the destination, the Villa Tugendhat, on the left.

Superb Residence with Scattered Wounds

Two of major residential works by Mies are the Barcelona Pavilion [1] and the Villa Tugendhat. They were completed at almost same time (in 1929). Mies was 43 then and in his most productive years.

These two representative works of the master architect of modern architecture; Barcelona Pavilion and Villa Tugendhat. The former was doomed to be destroyed within 1 year because it was the Pavilion for the Barcelona International Exhibition.

The latter escaped demolition though it was also unlucky. The Villa had a lot of ups and downs due to the changes in the control of the society.

Mies had a variety of possible clients from the leftwing and the rightwing. Eduard Fuchs[2], a leftwing historian, introduced Mr. and Mrs. Tugendhats to Mies.

The Tugendhats were young, rich, Jewish, business people and they were newlyweds.

---

[2]エードゥアルド・フックス
歴史家、ユダヤ人。著作『風俗の歴史』、『ヨーロッパ風刺画の歴史』などで名高い。

[2]**Eduard Fuchs**
Historian, Jewish. Famous for his publications such as "Illustrierte Sittengeschichte vom Mittelalter bis zur Gegenwart (History of Morality)" and "Caricatures of European People".

クライアントのトゥーゲントハット夫妻は、結婚したばかりの若くて富裕なユダヤの実業家一家。夫フリッツに妻グレーテ。グレーテの父親は富豪で、結婚祝いに新居を「娘の選んだ建築家に建てさせる」ことを約束していた。夫妻はミースの住宅作品を3軒見学し、その中でフックスの住んでいた元ペルルス邸に惹かれる。「広々とした空間と、清潔で簡素な形を持った近代的住宅」を希望し、建築家に伝えた。紆余曲折はあったが、彼らはこの建物を大変気に入り、幼い子供を育てながら生活を始める。

　しかしながら、第二次世界大戦が勃発、1939年にはヒトラーの軍隊がチェコスロバキアに侵攻することとなる。家具や建具そして建築金物の隅々にまで、ミースのアイデアが練り込まれたトゥーゲントハット邸は、わずか10年に満たない間に主を変える。ユダヤ人である建主は身の危険を察知、多くの同国人がアウシュビッツ送りになる状況下、南米に逃れる。

　「かつてユダヤ人の所有であった豪邸」が目立たないはずはない。最初はヒトラーの軍隊が接収。その後、個性的かつ秀逸な戦闘機の設計者として歴史に名を残すメッサーシュミット博士に住居として与えられる。ミリタリー・デザイン界の天才が、奇しくも建築界の大巨匠の自信作に住んだことになる。博士は意外にも広いリビングの空間を持て余し、いい加減な間仕切りで区切って使っていたとも伝えられる。

　しばらくしてドイツ軍の東部戦線が崩壊すると、ブルノにもロシア軍が進駐。今日では想像しにくいが、この住宅の大いなる特徴のひとつであるオニックスの壁の前で、兵隊たちが炉をつくって肉を焼いたという話が伝わっている。メインフロアをゆるやかに仕切る、マカッサル黒檀の存在感のゆたかな半円形平面の壁もいつの間にか失われた（略奪されたという説も）という。

　戦後はソ連共産党の所有→チェコ共産党の施設→バレエ学校にも転用された。トゥーゲントハット邸の大きな特徴のひとつである庭側の大型一枚ガラスの巨大可動サッシも、小割のものに変更された。玄関脇につくられた、メインフロアに至る半円形部分のある階段を囲う乳白色の曲面ガラスも、普通の横長窓のあるコンクリート壁に変わった。

　つまり、トゥーゲントハット邸は解体こそされなかったものの、時代に翻弄されその姿は満身創痍であった。

主要作品

1907年	リール邸
1922年	ガラスのスカイスクレーパー案（未実現）
1927年	ワイセンホーフ・シードルンク
1929年	バルセロナ・パビリオン
1930年	トゥーゲントハット邸
1951年	ファンズワース邸
1951年	レイクショアドライブ・アパートメント
1956年	IITクラウンホール
1958年	シーグラムビル

Significant Buildings

1907 Riehl House
1922 all-glass Friedrichstrasse skyscraper (unbuilt)
1927 Weissenhof Apartments
1929 Barcelona Pavillion
1930 Villa Tugendhat
1951 Farnsworth House
1951 LakeShoreDrive Apartments
1956 Crown Hall, IIT's School of Architecture
1958 Seagram Building

Fritz (husband) and Grete (wife). Grete's father was a millionaire and promised a wedding gift; a house designed by an architect she chose. The couple visited 3 houses by Mies and they liked the former Peris House, where Fuchs used to live. They requested a "modern residence with a large space and a simple shape" to the architect. Though there were twists and turns, the Tugendhats liked this building very much. They started their life and raising their children in this house.

However, WWII broke out and Hitler's army invaded Czechoslovakia in 1939. The Villa Tugendhat, where Mies expressed his ideas even with furniture, fittings and architectural hardware, changed its owner within just 10 years. The Jewish owners sensed danger and escaped to the South America, while many Jews were sent to Auschwitz.

The "luxurious previous Jewish residence" could not have a low profile. First Hitler's army took it over. It was then given to Dr. Messerschmitt, a renowned and unique warplane designer as a residence. By coincidence a genius of military design lived in a masterpiece of a great architect. There is a story that the living room was too large for Dr. Messerschmitt and he put up partition walls there.

After a while, the German eastern front was broken and the Russian army made an entry into Brno. They say the soldiers grilled meat in front of the onyx wall, one of the features of this house, though it is not easy to imagine such a situation now. The outstanding semicircular wall of Makassar ebony wood, loosely separating the main floor, was lost (some say "stolen") for some time.

In the postwar period, the Villa Tugendhat changed its owners from the Communist Party of the Soviet Union to the Communist of the Czechoslovakia and even to a ballet school. One of the greatest features of the house, large one plate glass with retractable sashes was replaced by smaller ones. The milky white curving glass around the strand stairway to the main floor beside the entrance was replaced by a concrete wall with a horizontally long window.

That is, the Villa Tugendhat was not destroyed, but was full of scars due to various social changes.

ミースの住宅スタイル

ミースの住宅は、時代の芸術や社会や技術に色濃く影響を受けながら大いなる変遷をする。

1：デビュー作「リール邸」を始めとする初期。この期間の作風は矩形平面に勾配屋根という伝統的様式を特徴とする。

2：デ・スティルに刺激を受け、壁が解体され、柱梁フレームの登場で壁が構造体の役目を逃れ、自由に配置される。バルセロナ・パヴィリオン、トゥーゲントハット邸、そして「子供のない夫婦の家（ベルリン建築展モデル住宅）」に、それらの手法の顕著な作例を見ることができる。

3：コートハウスは、後の世に北欧などの新興住宅地でかなり普及しているが、パイオニアたるミースの作品はいずれも計画案止まりのアンビルトであった。「3つの中庭をもつコートハウス」「ガレージを持つコートハウス」「ウルリッヒ・ラング邸」「フッペ邸」などが知られている。

4：アメリカ移住後のミースの仕事は、巨大建築にその比重を移行し、相対的に戸建住宅の仕事は減る。コートハウスの追求をした後であったが、アメリカの広大な敷地ではその意味が希薄となり、別の可能性の追求となる。この時期もアンビルトが多い中、構造フレームを外に並べ、2枚の水平スラブを支え、矩形の外皮は全部ガラスという究極の住宅「ファンズワース邸」に至る。

a ファン・ドゥースブルフの絵画『ロシア舞踊のリズム』、1918年
b レンガの田園郊外住宅計画、1923年（未実現）
c バルセロナ博覧会でのミースによるドイツ・パビリオン、1928～29年
d トゥーゲントハット邸の主要階（住居スペース）、1928～30年
e 子供のない夫婦の家、1931年
f フッペ邸、1935年（未実現）

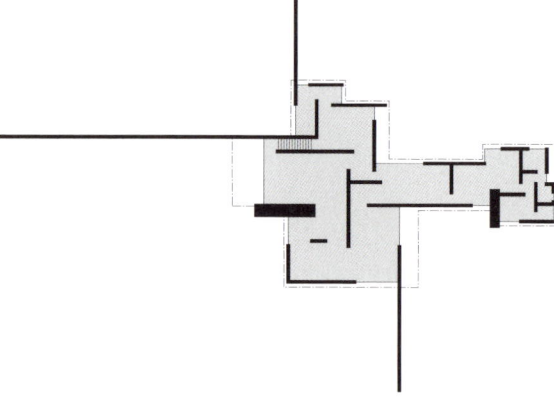

a Theo van Doesburg's painting *Rhythm of a Russian Dance*, 1918
b Mies's Brick Country House, 1923 (unbuilt)

Housing Styles of Mies

Housing designed by Mies was a great transition, and was influenced much by the society and technology of the era.

1. *His early years with the Riehl House, with which he made his debut. His style at this time was traditional with a rectangle plan and a pitched roof.*

2. *Inspired by de Stijl, walls were destroyed. Walls as structure were replaced by frames of columns and beams and therefore walls could be freely located. You can clearly see such characteristics in the Barcelona Pavilion, the Villa Tugendhat and the "residence for a childless couple (Berlin Architectural Exhibition Model House)."*

3. *All of the courthouses designed by Mies were not realized although such housing became popular in later years in new towns in Scandinavian countries and others. Court housings planned by Mies include "a courthouse with 3 courtyards," "a courthouse with a garage," "Ullrich Lang house" and "Huppe House"*

4. *After going to the USA, Mies gave greater importance to large architecture and, in comparison, less to detached houses. Although he had designed courthouses before, he pursued other possibilities because such houses have less significance in a larger country like the USA. He had many designs which remained unbuilt at this time too, however, he finally completed the "Farnsworth House." All the walls of this ultimate house were made of glass and two horizontal slabs were stabilized by the outside structural frame.*

c Mies's German Pavilion at Barcelona Exposition, 1928-9
d The main (living-area) floor of his Villa Tugendhat, 1928-30
e Mies's House for a childless Couple, 1931
f Hubbe House, 1935 (unbuilt)

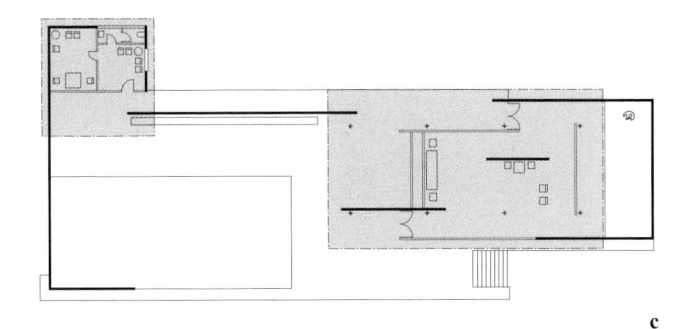

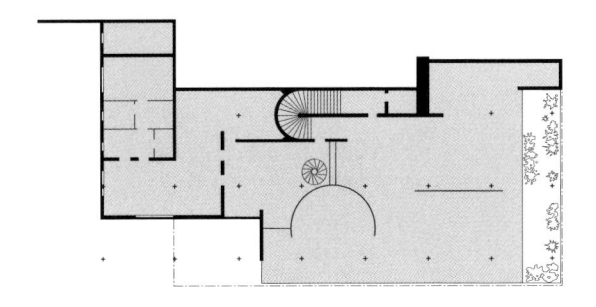

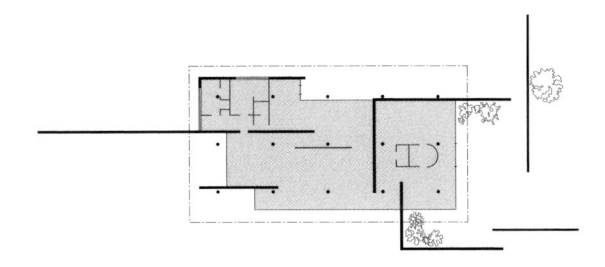

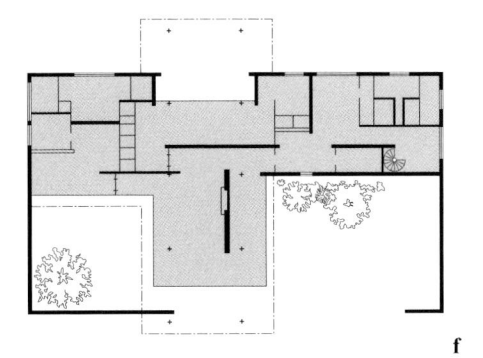

創建時の姿に復元、そして世界遺産へ

　1960年代に入ると、傷だらけで原形をとどめないトゥーゲントハット邸を元の状態に戻し、文化的な目的に使おうという活動が建築家フランティセック・カリヴォダの主導で始められる。
　1962年から69年にかけては子供病院のリハビリテーション・センターとして供用。1963年、「文化的モニュメント」に指定。1980年、ブルノ市の所有に。82〜85年、州の歴史的建造物再建委員会による復元工事が実施される。85〜93年、市へのVIPの訪問者のためのゲストハウスに。93年には市議会がトゥーゲントハット邸の文化的利用を決議。94年、ブルノ市博物館の管理下におかれ、一般公開が始まる。翌95年には国の文化モニュメントに指定。そして2001年には世界遺産指定となる。

出生地の地政学的座標

　祖父ヤコブ・ミース、父ミヒャエル・ミースはともに大理石細工師で、マントルピースや墓石を商っていた。1886年生まれのマリア・ルートヴィッヒ・ミヒャエル・ミースは、石に囲まれて育った。建築家としての石に関する格別のこだわりはこのころの環境に影響を受けている。
　職業訓練校で製図工としての教育を受けた後、漆喰装飾の実務についた後、建築家ブルーノ・パウルの事務所に勤務。その後1907年（21歳）に最初の事務所を構える。独立第一作でその才を認められた彼が企図したことは、改名であった。実はドイツ語のミース＝Miesは、「くだらない、ひどい」などの意味を持つ。これを建築家としての職能上プラスにならないと考えたのだ。
　彼は、母アマーリエ・ローエと父ミヒャエル・ミースの間に生まれた5人兄姉弟の末子であるルートヴィッヒ・ミースは、自らの姓名もデザインした。すなわち、ルートヴィッヒ・ミースの後に、母の優雅な旧姓「ローエ」を採用、オランダ貴族風の前置詞と定冠詞を付与し「ファン・デル・ローエ」を繋げたのだ。「レオナルド・ダ・ヴィンチ」が「ヴィンチ村出身のレオナルド」であるように、「高貴なローエ家にルーツを持つルートヴィッヒ・ミース」の意である。
　アーヘン出身で、ドイツ人たるミースが、ロケットの「フォン・ブラウン博士」や「フォン・ヒンデンブルク大統領」のようにドイツ語の「フォン」ではなく、「ファン・ゴッホ」や「ファン・ドゥースブルフ」（芸術運動デ・スティルの中心人物）、「フ

●シュレーダーハウス
G. T. リートフェルト作　1924年 ユトレヒト
デ・スティル派の典型的な色彩、赤、青、黄の三色に白、グレー、黒を織り交ぜた構成で、田の字型プランの西洋建築史上ユニークな住宅。2000年に世界遺産登録。

Schröder House
G. T. Rietveld, 1924, Utrecht Composed of typical 3 colors of de Stijl, red, blue and yellow and white, gray and black are added. This house has a 4-room type layout and is unique in Western architectural history. Registered on the World Heritages List in 2000.

オルタハウス
ヴィクトル・オルタ作　1901年
ブリュッセル
植物をモチーフとした有機的な曲線形状を鋳鉄で造り上げた内装に、柔らかな自然光が降り注ぐ。現在は、アール・ヌーヴォーに関する美術館として一般公開。2000年に世界遺産登録。

Horta House
Victor Horta, 1901, Brussels
A gentle light falls upon the interior decoration made of case iron in the curving shape of organic plants. This house is now open to public as a museum on art nouveau. Registered on the World Heritages List in 2000.

Restored to the Original Shape and to Be on the World Heritage List

Activities started with the initiative of Frantisek Kalivoda to restore and use the deteriorated Villa Tugendhat for cultural purposes in 1960s.

It was used as a rehabilitation center for a children's hospital from 1962 to 1969. In 1963, the housing was registered as a "Cultural Monument. " Then the villa came to belong to Brno city in 1980. The Historical Architecture Reconstruction Committee of the state implemented restoring construction. The residence was then a guest house for VIPs visiting the city from 1985 to 1993. In 1993, the city council passed a resolution that the Villa Tugendhat should be used for cultural purposes. In the following year, the house was under the surveillance of the Brno city museum open to public. The villa was registered as a national cultural monument in 1995 and as one of the UNESCO's World Heritages in 2001.

Geopolitical Position of Mies' Birthplace

His grandfather Jacob Mies and father Michael Mies were both marble workers and dealt with mantelpieces and gravestones. "Maria Ludwig Michael" Mies, born in 1886, grew up with stone. His specific commitment to stone as an architect was influenced by such circumstances.

After working on drafting at an industrial training school, he did professional practice on plaster decoration. Then, he worked at the office of architect Bruno Paul's. He opened the first office on his own in 1907, when he was 21 years old. His talent was recognized with his first work and he then planned to change his name. Actually, the word "Mies" means "rubbish" or "bad" in German. He thought this would not be good for his architectural profession.

Ludwig Mies, born the youngest of 5 brothers and sisters from their mother Amalie Rohe and father Michael Mies, designed his own name. That is, he put "Rohe," his mother's sophisticated name, after "Ludwig Mies. " He also chose a preposition and a definite article like a noble Dutch; "van der Rohe. " Just as "Leonardo da Vinci" meaning "Leonardo from the Vinci village," his name means "Ludwig Mies from the Rohe family. "

Mies was a German and born in Aachen. However, he used Dutch "van," as artists Van Eyck brothers, "Van Gogh" or "van Doesburg", not German "von," as Dr. von Braun famous for rocket designing or President von Hindenburg. There was a significant meaning to this.

ァン・アイク兄弟」（画家）のようにオランダ語の「ファン」を名乗ったことには深い意味がある。

　アーヘンは、8世紀建立、フランク王国のカール大帝の宮廷礼拝堂に増築した大聖堂のある門前町。ケルンの西60km、DB（ドイツ国鉄）で小一時間の距離にある。アーヘンの街は西側でオランダ国境とベルギー国境に接している。この街の地政学的位置が、ミースの改名とそのデザイン哲学に強くかかわる。

「ミース紀元元年」、同時代の建築家たち

　歴史上のある時期が、どのような時代であったかを概観するのに、同時代人を並べてみる手法がある。ミース、コルビュジェ、ライト、グロピウスの4人は「近代建築の4大巨匠」と呼ばれる。「巨匠」の一人として、建築界でそれまで試みられていなかったことを行い、後世に多大な影響を及ぼしたミースの生年である1886年を仮に「ミース元年」とすると、欄外の一覧のようになる。

　同時代人が並んだだけで、時代背景が立体的に浮かび上がる。ちなみにル・コルビュジェとミースとグロピウスは一時、ベーレンスの事務所の所員であった。ミースは、設計チーフであったグロピウスのもとで働いた時期がある。ル・コルビュジェの在籍期間はミースと重複していない。ル・コルビュジェはペレの事務所に在籍した時代もある。

　浮世絵の商いで勢いのあったパリの美術商ビングの店の名前『アール・ヌーヴォー』が、新たな芸術運動の名前として世界を席巻するのもミースは青年時代である。

　画家の影響という視点では、トゥーゲントハット邸も含め、「バルセロナ・パヴィリオン」やアメリカ移住後の「ファンズワース邸」に至るまで、ミースの住宅作品の壁の配置構成が、デ・スティルの中心人物であったファン・ドゥースブルフの抽象絵画にインスパイアされた様子が窺える。

　博覧会という形の情報発信にも注目する必要がある。1862年のロンドン博、1867年のパリ博、1873年のウィーン博と欧州人の間に日本文化への関心が異常な高まりを見せる。併せて米国では、1876年フィラデルフィア建国百年博における2棟の日本建築、さらに1893年シカゴのコロンビア博における日本館（鳳凰殿）が大いなる評判を呼ぶなど日本建築が西洋世界に濃厚に認知された時期にも当たっている。

同時代の建築家たち

オットー・ワグナー（1841年）
−45年

ヴィクトル・オルタ
−25年

フランク・ロイド・ライト
−19年

ペーター・ベーレンス
−18年

アドルフ・ロース
−16年

オーギュスト・ペレ
−12年

ブルーノ・タウト
−6年

ワルター・グロピウス
−3年

ミース・ファン・デル・ローエ
1886年生まれ

エリッヒ・メンデルゾーン
+2年

ル・コルビュジェ
+3年

G. T. リートフェルト
+3年

Architects of the Same Period

Otto Wagner (1841)
　−45
Victor Horta
　−25
Frank Lloyd Wright
　−19
Peter Behrens
　−18
Adolf Loos
　−16
Auguste Perret
　−12
Bruno Taut
　−6
Walter Gropius
　−3
Mies van der Rohe
　born in 1886
Erich Mendelsohn
　+2
Le Corbusier
　+3
G. T. Rietvelt
　+3

Aachen has a cathedral, an annex of the imperial court bethel of the Charles the Great of Francia. The city is located 60km west from Koln and it is about 1 hour distance by DB (German national railway). The west part of Aachen meets Holland and Belgium. The geopolitical position of this city had a great influence on the name change and design philosophy of Mies.

Mies Era, Architects of the Same Period

You can make a list of the people of the same period to overview a certain era in history. Mies, Le Corbusier, Wright and Gropius are called "4 pioneering masters of 'modern' architecture. " Mies, one of the masters, did previously unexplored things in the architectural world and is a great influence even now. Set 1886, when he was born, as the beginning of the "Mies Era" then, make a list in the margin.

Just a comparison of the people of the same period makes the social background very clear.

In this connection, Le Corbusier, Mies and Gropius had working experience at the office of Peter Behrens. Mies worked for Gropius, who was a design chief. Le Corbusier and Mies did not work there at the same time. Le Corbusier worked at the office of Auguste Perret too.

Samuel Bing, a fine art dealer in Paris, was dealing with Ukiyoe, Japanese woodblock prints, and getting ahead in business. "Art Nouveau," the name of his shop was known around the world as an international style of art. Mies was in his youth then.

Regarding the influence made by painters, you can find inspiration from van Doesburg, who was among the main activists of de Stijl, in the wall compositions of the residential works of Mies, including the Villa Tugendhat, the "Barcelona Pavilion" and the "Farnsworth House" in the USA.

Attention should be paid to the transmission of information as a form of an exposition. Japanese culture was receiving increasing attention among Europeans during the London expo in 1862, the Paris expo in 1867 and Vienna expo in 1873. In addition, that period was when Japanese architecture was widely recognized in the western world, including 2 Japanese buildings at the Philadelphia nation-building 100 anniversary expo in 1876 and Japanese pavilion; Ho-O-Den (Phoenix Hall) at the Colombia expo in Chicago in 1893.

モダニストの共通点

　近代建築の4大巨匠の中で、とりわけ饒舌であったル・コルビュジェ以外は、著作がほとんど知られていない。しかしながらミースが際立っているのは、モダニズム建築の精神を「Less is more」というわかりやすい教条で表現したことによる。

　巨匠たちに共通するのは、「Less is more」の精神のほか、機能主義であり、脱装飾であり、形態的には陸屋根であり、壁式（組積造）からの離脱であった。すなわち「建築が重力（建物の荷重）を負担する壁がなくても成立すること」、「四隅に壁が存在しなくても建築が構成できること」をそれぞれの表現方法で実現したのが彼らであった。

　「壁構造の呪縛からの解放」という視点でミースの建築の時代背景を整理してみると、次の三点が考えられる。

(1) 歴史主義もしくは新古典主義（主としてグリーク・リバイバル）が挙げられる。活動の場をベルリンに移した青年ミースが心酔していた新古典主義の旗手カール・フリードリヒ・シンケル[※3]の一連の作品、とりわけ博物館島の旧博物館（アルテス・ムゼウム[※4]）の列柱に象徴的な「壁から独立して存在する柱による構造体」というヒントが存在した。

(2) 日本建築（主として東屋や舞殿系の壁なし建築、鳳凰堂などの高床式建築）への重大な関心。

(3) 欧米における浮世絵絵画の大ブームがあった。

　柱と柱の上に横に架かる梁の構造をもつギリシア建築以後、西洋建築の歴史において「壁がなくては建築が存在し得ない」という常識が連綿と続いた。20世紀になってル・コルビュジェが「ドミノシステム」を提唱、これが「近代建築5原則」に発展結実することになる。しかしながら、実は日本建築ではあたりまえの概念であった。巨匠たちが「日本建築にインスパイアされた」と告白したところで彼らの名声がいささかも揺らぐとはないのだが、彼らはそれをしていない。

　トゥーゲントハット邸における独立柱の存在は、フル・ハイトのガラス面（温室のある南面と、市街地を見下ろす西面）を可能にした魔法の杖である。壁から荷重を支える役割を解放してくれる柱を、ランダムに見える壁と併用することで、それまで世界のどこにも存在しなかった建築を生み出した。

　ミースはほぼ同時期に、スペイン、バルセロナとチェコのブルノで双生児のようにコンセプトの良く似た二つの作品を世に送り出した。

　バロック、ロココ、アール・ヌーヴォーという近世西洋の装飾至上の伝統への反動、その反動の主流となった新古典主義か

[※3] カール・フリードリヒ・シンケル 建築家。(1781-1841) 18西紀ドイツの新古典主義建築を代表する建築家。作風は、ギリシア建築を倣っているが幾何学的で端正なデザインは、モダニズムに通じている。

[※3] **Karl Friedrich Schinkel**
Architect (1781-1841)
Architect representing the Neoclassicism architecture of Germany in the 18th century. His geometric and clean-cut style, although along the line of Greek architecture, is in tune with Modernism.

Common Ground for Modernists

Many of the publications by the 4 pioneering masters of "modern" architecture are not known except for the ones of Le Corbusier, who was very fluent among them. However, Mies is outstanding in that he expressed the spirit of modernism architecture with the simple dogma, "Less is more."

The common ground for these masters includes functionalism, less ornamentation, flat roofs, the landing off from wall construction (masonry construction) and the spirit of "less is more." That is, they expressed respectively in their way; "architecture can stand without bearing walls" and "architecture can be composed without surrounding walls."

The social backgrounds of Mies' architecture can be summarized regarding "release from the curse of wall construction" as below.

(1) Historicism or Neoclassicism (mainly Greek Revival). Young Mies moved his main place of business to Berlin and he was fascinated with the work of Karl Friedrich Schinkel[※3], a standard-bearer of Neoclassicism. There was a hint of "structure with columns not with walls," in a series of works done by Schinkel, especially a line of columns of the Old Museum (Altes Museum[※4]) on the Museum Island.

(2) Great interest in Japanese architecture (mainly architecture without walls such as an arbor or a temple for dancing, or a raised-floor architecture such as the Phoenix Hall.)

(3) Big Boom of Ukiyoe, Japanese woodblock prints in Western countries.

Since the Greek architecture, which has the structure with horizontal beams on columns, it had seemed common sense that architecture could not exist without walls. Le Corbusier, in the 20th century, proposed the "Domino" system, which lead to the "five points of modern architecture." However, this was a natural concept in Japanese architecture. The masters did not confess that they were inspired by Japanese architecture though such a confession would not abase their reputation.

The independent columns of the villa are like magic wands, which enabled glass surfaces standing at full height (the southern façade with a conservatory and the western façade looking down the city area.) Mies made unprecedented architecture using columns releasing walls from weight and walls that look random.

Mies completed twin works, almost like carbon copies at almost the same time; one in Barcelona, Spain and the other in Brno, Czech.

Adolf Loos[※5] turned his back on the modern Western tradition of respecting decoration, such as Baroque, Rococo and Art Nouveau. He

[※4]アルテス・ムゼウム
シンケル作 1930年 ベルリン。博物館島にあり、現在はギリシア、ローマの芸術作品を主に展示。

[※4] **Altes Museum**
1930, Berlin, designed by Schinkel
Located on the Museumsinsel (museum island), it now mainly displays Greek and Roman art works.

らも距離を置いたアドルフ・ロース※5。新たな地平を模索する動きは、『装飾は犯罪』と言った彼によって近代建築の潮流が確立し始める。

イメージを実現する突出した建設費

　工事費に関する資料を発掘したサンドラ・ホーニー（Sandra Horney）によると、この住宅の工事費は「当時のかなり贅沢なアパートの住戸8戸分のコストがかかっていた」と言われている。この記述、当初は誇張だと思っていた。しかしながら、現物を仔細に眺めてみると、荒唐無稽な誇張表現でないことに気づく。『MIES VAN DER ROHE』（TASCHEN）によれば、コルビュジェの「サヴォア邸」の約10倍の建築費とある。
その中でも建材の使い方が突出している。一般に、石材、とりわけ高価なオニックス系の大理石の場合には、9〜20ミリ厚程度にスライスして躯体やブロック積みの下地の上に、セメント・ペーストや接着剤で貼り付ける。ところがここトゥーゲントハット邸のリビングでは、高価なモロッコ産オニックスが、高さ3.17mの天井まで、幅約1.2m、厚さ約70ミリの1枚板の5枚構成で間仕切壁となっている。前掲書では「このオニックスだけで並みの住居が1軒建つ」と表現している。工業製品とは違い、素材の材齢が千万から億年単位となる大理石に、「究極のシンプル」を追求した室内における"風格の要素"を期待したのではないかと想像される。石に関するミースの格別のこだわりは、祖父から父と2代続いた「石屋」の血筋であろう。

　玄関回りと階段室の明り取りの乳白色のガラスは、1枚が幅2.3m高さ3mでエッチング処理、しかも曲面加工と高価格な要素のかたまりである。

　ブルノの市街地を遥かに見下ろす西斜面側のガラス面の延長は24m弱。それを5等分して、そのうちの2枚、概ね一枚の幅4.8m×高さ3.2mのガラス面が、電動でそっくり下階の壁の中に引き込まれ、床から天井までが100％の完全開放となる。現状は幅2.4mのガラス2枚をシリコンコーキングで繋いでいるが、オリジナルは1枚ガラスであったかもしれない。その時代に大型ガラスを作る技術はヨーロッパにあった。ほぼ同時代のサヴォア邸の最大のガラスは1枚が2.8m×4.6mある。一般見学者には、ましてや冬季には、電動窓のデモをしないとのことだが、特別に開けて見せてくれた。外は雪景色であった。「風流とは寒きものなり」という我が国の諺を現地にプレゼントしたいほどに寒さよりも感動が優る。

ミューラー邸
アドルフ・ロース作　1930年
プラハ
ロースハウス（1910年）に並ぶ彼の代表作。真っ白な外観からは想像もできない装飾的な内部空間は、ラウムプランと呼ばれる微妙に段差を付けた空間で構成されている。

Villa Müller
Designed by Adolf Loos, 1930, Prague
One of Loos' best works along with Looshaus (1910). Its decorative interior space, unimaginable from the snow-white appearance, is composed of Raumplan, space with subtly different levels.

西側の居間。

Living room on the west

※5 アドルフ・ロース
建築家。オーストリア生まれ
(1870-1933)。
ドレスデンで学んだ後、アメリカに渡り実用的なデザインを学び帰国。当時全盛の装飾主義を否定し、機能主義の主張をする。代表作ロースハウスは、装飾をそぎ落としたモダニズム建築の先駆的作品。×

※5 **Adolf Loos**
Architect. Born in Austria (1870-1933).
After studying in Dresden, Loos mastered practical design in the USA. He asserted Functionalism, denying Decorationism, which was at its peak then. His major work Looshaus, without decoration, is a pioneer in Modernism architecture.

even distanced himself from Neoclassicism, which became the mainstream of such a backlash. Loos, who said "ornamentation is a crime," established a new stream of Modern architecture searching for a new horizon.

Outstanding Construction Fees to Realize Images

According to Sandra Horney, who found the documents on the construction fees, this residence was said to be "8 times as expensive as highly luxurious apartments at that time. " This was thought to be an exaggeration. But it will not seem to be a silly exaggeration, if you examine the housing carefully. "MIES FAN DER ROHE" (TASCHEN) says that the construction fees of the villa were about 10 times as much as those of the Villa Savoye by Le Corbusier.

Especially, outstanding is the use of stone materials. They usually attach stone, in particular, expensive onyx, marble, sliced at about a thickness of 9-20mm, upon the surface of a building frame or block masonry with cement paste or glue. However, expensive Moroccan onyx is luxuriously used in the living room of this villa. Five panels are used as a partition wall and each panel is about 70mm (thickness) ×1.2m (width)×3.17m (height). The book cited above indicates "with the price of this onyx, you can buy a usual house. " Marble can be 10 to 100 million years old, different from industrial products, and Mies might have thought such marble to be a "stately element. " Particular preferences of Mies for stone would have derived from his "stone artisan" blood for 2 generations from his grandfather and his father.

The milk white glass around the entrance and the window at the stairway is full of expensive elements such as a large plate of 2.3m (width)×3m (height), etching finish and curving treatment.

The glass surface on the western façade, looking down at Brno city in the distance, has nearly 24m long. There are 5 plates, each of which is about 4.8m (width)×3.2m (height). Two of these 5 plates are retracted by electricity into the lower floor wall and there is a full height opening from the ceiling to the floor. A pair of 2.4m glass is connected to each other with silicon caulking, but the original might have been one plate of glass of the whole size of 4.8m. There was a technique to make a huge glass plate in Europe. The largest glass at the Villa Savoye, of almost the same period, is 2.8m×4.6m. They won't show a demonstration of the electric window for ordinary visitors, especially during the winter time, but they will on special occasions. There was snowy scenery outside. I wanted to give them a Japanese proverb as a gift "an elegant aestheticism can be cold," because I was more moved than cold.

ダイニングのゾーンの直径6.9mの半円形構成も圧巻。インドネシア産のマカッサル黒檀を厚練りしたブックマッチの連続模様で構成される12のパーツから成る。重量感溢れる厚さ70ミリの間仕切りも圧倒的な存在感を示している。

　地下2階には、電動の巨大ガラス窓をそっくり収める格納スペースと駆動装置、複数の倉庫、洗濯室などのほか、スチーム輻射熱暖房のためのボイラー室、さらに（二重装備だが）温風を吹き出すセントラルヒーティングの機械室が大きな面積を占める。

　ヨーロッパの気候では冬の暖房は必須であるが、夏季の冷房は、現在でも4つ星ホテル以上でないと装備されることは少ない。突出して広く、格別の高級建材をふんだんに組み合わせた住居は、空調も至れり尽くせりとなっている。ボイラー室の北側に並ぶ小室群は冷房と加湿のためのものである。

　さらに、トゥーゲントハット邸のなかでの贅沢な要素として特筆されるのが、書斎・居間ゾーンの南側に設けられた温室である。幅2.6m、奥行き14.5mのスペースに、シダ系、ゴムノキ系の観葉植物が置かれている。伝統的に上流階級の城郭や巨大邸宅の「標準装備」であった温室は、ここトゥーゲントハット邸でも設けられた。それは、フルハイトの巨大ガラスで覆われたモダニズム建築の記念碑の一要素として、その存在を主張している。

　冬季でも日照がある場合には文字通りの温室になるが、雨の日、雪の日、曇りの日や夜間には暖房が必要。床面のガラリからの温風吹出しと、観葉植物を乗せるトラバーチン台の下に低く、横長に設けられたスチーム輻射熱暖房のラジエターが用意されている。

現在は、トゥーゲントハット邸の模型がテーブル上に置かれている。本来は、食堂。

This was originally a dining room and there is now a model of the Villa Tugendhat on the table.

写真奥の温室に並ぶ植木鉢の下部にラジエターが用意。余分なインテリアを配置しない美学が、住宅全体に徹底している。

There is a radiator under the plant pots in the rear of the conservatory An aesthetic of avoiding unnecessary interior decoration covers the whole of the residence.

A semicircular composition with a diameter of 6.9m is also a sight to see in the dining room. It is made of 12 parts; book matches pattern of thick Makassar ebony made in Indonesia. The partition wall with a thickness of 70mm appears heavy and has a great presence.

Much of the space on the 2nd basement floor is occupied by the storage for the electric huge glass window and driving gear, several storages, the laundry room, the boiler room for steam radiation heaters, and the machine room for central heating with hot air (double equipment).

Heating in winter is a must in the European climate. However, it is rare to have air conditioning in summer except for the hotels with more than four stars. This villa, exceptionally large and with notably expensive materials, has overwhelming air conditioning too. The small rooms along the boiler room on the north side are for cooling and humidification.

Worthy of note regarding another luxury element is a conservatory in the south of the reading and living area. There are leafy plants in a space of 2.6m (width)×14.5m (depth) such as ferns and rubber trees. A conservatory, which traditionally used to be standard equipment of a chateau or a mansion of the upper social class, was made in this Villa Tugendhat. This has a presence as a certain element of the monument of Modernism architecture covered with full-height huge glass plates.

This can literally be a conservatory even in winter whenever there is sunlight. But you need heating on rainy days, snowy days, cloudy days or at night. There are horizontal and lowly set radiators at the ventilator on the floor and under the travertine table for leafy plants.

着工当時の貴重な写真。

Significant photo at the construction of the Villa Tugendhat.

"Less is more"の一頂点

　ミースのアメリカ亡命後の作品、完全無柱空間のファンズワース邸[※6]（1951）、校舎スケールに翻訳されたイリノイ工科大学のクラウンホール（1956）、現代風超高層の「教科書」シーグラムビル（1958）、ユニバーサルスペースの到達点、ベルリンの新国立ギャラリー[※7]（1968）などいずれも一世を風靡した世界的な話題作であり、地球上の至るところに夥しい数の亜流建築の発生を誘発した。このトゥーゲントハット邸を見ていると、これら後世の珠玉の作品群が透けて見える。

　トゥーゲントハット邸の外観は、今日的な感覚からすると、私たちにとっては、ほとんど違和感のない形態である。しかしながら創建時に思いを馳せれば、ブルノ郊外の高台の高級住宅地で、レンガ積み外壁に勾配屋根の建物群の中にあって、白く横に長い、外部に装飾的な一切の記号をまとわない陸屋根の大型住宅は、どれほどの衝撃を持って迎えられたことであろう。

　バロック、ロココ、新古典（歴史）主義、アール・ヌーヴォー、ベルエポック様式等々、「空白恐怖」に近いほど、西洋人の遺伝子に書き込まれた装飾の豊かな伝統風景の中で"Less is more"の出現は大事件であった。

　約130km南のウイーンで、1910年、アメリカ帰りの建築家・アドルフ・ロースが王宮のゲート正面に、装飾の衣を脱ぎ捨てたかのような「ロースハウス」を建て、ウイーン市民を震撼させたその時の衝撃に似たものがあったはずである。

　「装飾は犯罪である」とまで言い切ったロースの作品の中にも、モダニズム以降の建築教育を経た私たちには、それでもまだ装飾的要素が見て取れる。ロースより13年歳下のグロピウスや16年歳下のミースが行った創作は、"Less is more"というよりもほとんど"Zero is more"と言えるほどの究極のシンプルであった。

　トゥーゲントハット邸は約80年前に完成したとは思えないほど、今日、我々の目で見ても新鮮である。それだけの予言・予知能力を備えた、飛びぬけた才能による現代建築の貴重な記念碑となっている。ユトレヒトの「シュレーダー邸」、ブリュッセルの「オルタ邸」と並ぶ、個人住宅の世界遺産指定も、まさにそのあたりが評価されたものである。

[※6] **ファンズワース邸**
1951年　イリノイ
イリノイに週末別荘として建てられたもので、8本のスチールH型鋼に支持されていて、外壁はすべてガラスで構成。2003年にオークションに出され、ナショナルトラストが取得し、現在、世界遺産に登録。

[※6] **Farnsworth House**
1951, Illinois
This house was constructed as a weekend second house in Illinois. This is supported by 8 H-shaped steel columns and all the walls are glass. The National Trust purchased the house at an auction in 2003 and the house is now registered on the World Heritages List.

ブルノ市美術館とバウハウス・アーカイブのご好意に感謝いたします。

Peak of "Less is More"

The works after Mies fled to the USA are the topical, worldwide, predominant ones; Farnsworth House[*6] (1955): a totally column-free space; Crown Hall, IIT's School of Architecture (1956): a translation into the scale of school; Seagram Building (1958): a modern skyscraper "textbook"; New National Gallery in Berlin [*7](1968); with its goal of universal space. There have been countless epigones of these buildings. You can see these superb works that come through the Villa Tugendhat.

The appearance of the Villa Tugendhat is not uncomfort to us. , However, this villa would have been shocking at the time of its completion. A long, white mansion, with a flat roof, having no decorative signs outside, on a hill in Brno, in an exclusive residential district of brick with pointed roofs.

The appearance of "Less is More" was a real accident in the traditional context of rich decoration in the DNA of Western people through Baroque, Rococo, Neoclassicism (Historicism), Art Nouveau, Belle Epoque, and so on. Such preferences were almost a "blank-phobia."

In Vienna, about 130km to the south there must have been a similar astonishment among Viennese when Adolf Loos returning from the USA built, in front of the royal palace, the "Looshaus," as if it had thrown away all its decoration. .

We, who were trained under the architectural education after Modernism, can find some decorative elements even in the works of Loos who said "ornamentation is a crime." Gropius was younger than Loos by 13 years and Mies was younger by 16 years. They created buildings in an ultimately simple way. It was not just "Less is More" but more like "Zero is More."

The Villa Tugendhat remains fresh to us now though it was completed about 80 years ago. It is a spectacular monument of Modern architecture by a splendid talent with the ability to predict and foresee. Probably that is exactly why this house was registered on the list of World Heritages as an individual residence along with the "Schröder House" in Utrecht and the "Horta House" in Brussels.

[*7]ドイツ新国立美術館邸
1968年　ベルリン
一辺64.8mの鉄の大屋根が8本の十字柱によって支えられ、その中に中心軸を同じくして約50mの総ガラス張りのホールがある。実際の美術館としての機能のほとんどは地下に収められている。

[*7] **New National Gallery in Berlin**
1968, Berlin
The large square steel roof with a side of 64.8m is lifted up by 8 cross-shaped columns. The wholly glazed hall with a side of 50m is located under the roof. Most of the functional spaces of the museum are located underground.

By courtesy of Museum of the City of Brno and Bauhaus-Archiv Berlin.

Photos 宮本和義
写真家。1941年上海生まれ。1964年から建築分野、旅分野で活動。著書に『近代建築再見』(エクスナレッジ)、『古寺彩彩』(JTB)『近代建築散歩』(小学館)『サヴォア邸』(バナナブックス) など多数。

Text 栗田 仁
建築家。1949年生まれ。名古屋大学大学院修士課程修了。常葉学園大学造形学部、英和学院短大の非常勤講師。著書に『街はいつでも上機嫌』(静岡新聞社)『LRTが街を変える』(都市文化社)『オルタハウス』(バナナブックス) 他。

Photos Kazuyoshi Miyamoto
Photographer
Born in Shanghai in 1941
Since 1964, he has been taking
architectural and travel photographs.

Jin Kurita
Architect
Guest lecturer at Tokai University &
Tokoha University.　Born in 1949
Graduated from Nagoya University;
1975, MA in Architecture

撮影	宮本和義 ©
執筆	栗田仁 ©
翻訳	牧尾晴喜 [スタジオOJMM] ©
編集	石原秀一
	大石雄一朗
デザイン	堀井知嗣
図版	松尾茂男
印刷・製本	(株)新晃社
制作協力	アトリエM5
	森本京治 [M4建築設計室]
	ブルノ市美術館
	バウハウスアーカイブ
	東京大学工学部建築学科
	チェコ観光局(東京)
	Veronika Kristova
	Libor Teplý

Photos	© Kazuyoshi Miyamoto
Text	© Jin Kurita
Translation	© Haruki Makio (Studio OJMM)
Chief Editor	Shuichi Ishihara
Staff Editor	Yuichiro Oishi
Design	Tomotsugu Horii
Drafting	Shigeo Matsuo
Printer	Shinkohsha Co.,Ltd.
Special Thanks	atelier M5
	kyouji Morimoto (M4)
	Museum of the City of Brno
	Bauhaus-Archiv Berlin
	Department of Architecture,
	Faculty of Enjineering,the University
	of Tokyo
	Czech Republic Tourism Board (Tokyo)
	Veronika Kristova
	Libor Teplý

トゥーゲントハット邸
1930 チェコ
ミース・ファン・デル・ローエ
2008年6月28日発行
ISBN978-4-902930-16-0 C3352
発行者：石原秀一
発行所：バナナブックス ©
〒151-0051東京都渋谷区千駄ヶ谷5-17-15
TEL. 03-5367-6838 FAX. 03-5367-4635
URL: http://bananabooks.cc/

Villa Tugendhat
1930 Czech
Mies van der Rohe
28/6/2008 Publishing
ISBN978-4-902930-16-0 C3352
Publisher:Shuichi Ishihara
© Banana Books
5-17-15 Sendagaya Shibuya-ku, Tokyo, 151-0051 Japan
Tel. +81-3-5367-6838 Fax. +81-3-5367-4635
URL: http://bananabooks.cc/

2008 BananaBooks, Printed in Japan
All rights reserved
Any books with missing and/or misplaced pages will be replaced.